Hurricane

Shraddha Mehta

BookLeaf
Publishing

Presentation by *BookLeaf Publishing*

Web: www.bookleafpub.com

E-mail: info@bookleafpub.com

ISBN: 9789357610841

First edition 2023

DEDICATION

To my family,

I miss you Moti Mummy...

ACKNOWLEDGEMENT

I would like to acknowledge and thank my family and friends who listened to me drafting poems and dealt with how stressed I was when completing this challenge. This was a long time coming and thank you all for your patience and love. I appreciate all the wonderful people in my life and I am so lucky to call you my loved ones, you know who you are!

PREFACE

One small flutter of a butterfly's wings can cause a hurricane on the other side of the world…

~ The Butterfly Effect

New Beginnings

Your heart beats its own rhythm;
Your mind speaks its own fears.
Your existence immersed in chaos,
As new beginnings loom.

It stands in front of you;
Tall, big, and powerful.
The feeling of the unknown
can be eradicated with one step.

You take in the people,
All with coals for eyes
And tight-lipped smiles.
Wondering: Will this be you?

The roar of destruction,
Heavy machinery whirring,
As they demolish the old;
Hoping to replace with the new.

Taking deep breaths,
Gripping office bags.
Your heels press painfully;
Taking a small courageous step.

Towards the building,
With faceless people.
A place you will call home
For the duration of the job.

A Devi is Born

Embracing her womb affectionately in her arms,
She knew in her heart that her love was eternal.
Maternal instincts were starting to brew;
And a willingness to tackle all evil
To protect her little Angel.

'My Jaan' she beamed, swaying around;
Glistening with a joyful glee.
'My love for you will never waver,
Come storms and hurricanes alike,
I will always be by your side.'

Her husband kisses her forehead,
Thankful that his little family will be complete.
An introduction of an Angel boy,
Will fill the serene home with light
And a new innocence of life.

A looming question crosses her mind,
'Son? What if I have a beti?'
Her heart skips a beat, dreading his response;
A ghost of a threat. He says,
'You do not want to know.'

All colour falls, the world seems dark grey;
A cloud of anxiety pulsating every day.
She cocoons in herself, praying for a son;
For the sake of her unborn child,
And a destiny of unnecessary strife.

At last she snapped, like a twig flailing,
A glimmer of courage peeps in between.
'She wouldn't be a curse,
She won't bring us down;
I, unlike you, would love her with all my heart.'

She was met with aggression,
Red. Hot. Rage.
She protectively wrapped her universe;
And willingly turned her back;
to welcome the searing pain of his attacks.

An angel arrived followed by a blinding white light;
An epitome of innocence but she was ultimately torn;
For she knew this was only the beginning,
Of a lifetime of torment.
Because despite all her prayers, a Devi was born.

Glossary:
Jaan: a term of endearment (e.g. darling)
Beti: Daughter
Devi: Goddess

Dark Dates

Sharp blades,
Pain fades.
Searing skins,
Hot dates.

He was dangerous,
Her life? Adventurous.
Controlling passion,
Proceed with caution.

His hand coils,
Her neck strains.
Hatred radiates,
A love-filled embrace.

She welcomes the feeling,
Of heavy breathing,
Of unstoppable bleeding,
Slowly killing.

Rain

Rain,
Freefalling.

Washing,
Her existence.

Red taints her hand,
A shadow of pain.

Blood soaks her thigh,
And wetness under her eye.

Throat dry,
Choking up.

And lifelessly she falls,
Like the rain.

Epitome of Bliss

Her eyes sparkle;
In face of simple pleasures.
A fury of tingling laughter,
And ear-to-ear smiles.

Her insides warm,
In sheer joy
As she comprehends
Her blessings.

Some may think,
She is truly happy.
She glows like she is;
The epitome of bliss.

Hidden beneath it all,
A dark cloud of despair.
Her dirty little secret,
Ashamed to be let out.

She cloaks her darkness,
With the pretense of light.
Hoping her lie will somehow;
Turn into her real truth.

Dark clouds can't stay hidden for long.
An obvious thunder unmasks.
The crackle of lightning
And a brewing of the storm.

It engulfs her,
Until she is drowning.
Her own misery,
Slowly unveiling.

Surrounded

She was surrounded,
By sheer ecstasy.
The universe on paper
And her reason to live.

Her heart beats,
As one with the words.
Her eyes swallow,
Devouring pages whole.

Her nose willingly dives,
Into the rusty scent.
Her toothy smile,
Mumbles soulfully.

Her hair curtains,
Cocooning around.
As her being envelops,
In a blanket of calm.

She is surrounded,
by an oasis of safe.
She found the feeling,
Of heaven on earth.

The Dreaded Walk

Getting ready to leave,
The sun slowly setting.
Held back by millions
Of concerned questions.

She sighs as the words pass by,
Eyes rolling, clocks ticking.
She huffs and leaves,
a cloud of annoyance.

Walking alone is not a sin,
It can be safe.
Dark trees surround,
An eerie feel.

She shivers in instinct,
And scans around.
A tingling fear,
Slowly consumes.
Her hands wring,
Her eyebrows knit.
She takes deep breaths
As she passes the lake.

'It's nothing'
She consoles,

Irrational fear grows,
More, more, more.

A shadow jumps,
Her screams pierce.
Heart pounding as she
Studies her attacker.

Laughing in relief,
She pulls them close.
Hugging them tightly,
All angst melting.

Nothing to worry about,
Just a dear friend.
The idea of unease,
Unnecessarily fuelled her.

The dreaded walk
Was no more.
All in her head,
And from what she was told.

Burning Trust

Her trust is strong;
Never wavers.

They say once broken,
It cannot be whole again.
But not hers.

No skeptic or games,
Just white pureness.

She is like a gold prize;
People come to her,
From far and wide.

They want to reap her;
Of her niceness,
And giving nature.

She's not dumb,
Her eyes see the truth.

She knows it all,
Yet she chooses to believe.

Holding onto hope,
Gripping tightly.

Not ready to see.
The evil beyond.

Flames surround,
Courtesy of her friends.
Burning her like a knife.

Yet,
She believes.
With fiery determination.

The Call of the Void

Everyone has a voice in their head;
Bickering away,
With a million things to say.

Sometimes you just want it to
SHHH.
Shut up.

It's frustrating,
The evil thoughts it brings.
You want to believe;
You don't mean it.

How easy it would be to be bad,
Rob someone,
Murderous intentions,
Jump off a cliff…

The taunting haunts you,
Like a broken record.
The voice plays on.

You know deep down;
You won't act on it,
Yet those silly desires
Infiltrate your soul.

This is;
The call of the void.

Speak Up

Standing up there,
High and mighty,
The fleeting moment
Of absolute and complete power.

All those eyes,
Wide and anticipating;
Waiting for you to speak,
Hanging onto every word.

Your influence like no other,
The authority oozing off you,
Like a purple vapour;
Dangerous.

A dark sense of unease,
As you contemplate.
Evil thoughts infiltrate,
Your little puppets.

As you speak,
Your evil master plans.
They sinisterly smile,
To follow your whim.

Influence is powerful,
And sometimes all-destroying.
You stop yourself,
Thinking about the damage.

Your power comes with responsibility,
A privilege to be heard.
To be a voice for those who need it,
And spread some good.

The options lay in front of you,
Both very tempting;
The choice is clear,
Are you willing to take it?

Dance Away

Dance;
One word;
One emotion.

It excites me,
Supports me;
Gets me through.

The way my body moves,
Like a mere ripple in the water,
Drowning me without complaints.

The steady thump of the music,
Ignites all my nerves,
A gripping rhythm.

The slight hint of freedom,
Tingles on the tip of my tongue.
Like a cloud of paradise.

The salty smells surround,
Proof of rapid movements;
Yet, oddly serene.

The world spins around me,
As if dancing with me.

Supporting my obsession.

Dance;
My everything.
More than life.

To Your Core

The bright, beautiful sun,
Dies every day.
Just like you:
Every single day.

Sometimes the hope,
For a happy ending is strong.
You wait uselessly;
For what can never be.

You wait for the pain to end,
The loss and destruction.
Change that should be;
But never is.

Change is everywhere;
Just not the good kind.
Malicious intentions
Are fulfilled.,

Your heartbreak,
Is indescribable.
Only your core knows;
The pain of extinction.

You choose to rise;
Like the sun does.
To witness it again;
Feel the heat.

You survive another day,
Yet,
Like the sun;
You die again.

Lies

Thoughts are lost,
Lies are told,
In the myriad of human minds,
Two souls are found.

Lies get lost,
Lies get told,
Those lies kill hearts,
And apparently their souls.

Like a lifeless doll,
Those hearts beat,
Without purpose,
Love retreats.

Love has no place to grow,
To flourish,
Lies are toxic,
And innocents get punished.

Her heart beats,
Black tar.
Tainted by the lies,
Of her time.

Guardian Angel

Strangers,
Across the street.
They live close,
Yet, do not talk.

In times of trouble,
The other is forgotten,
In times of joy,
Invitations are not extended.

Blinded,
By the bright lights.
Captured,
By the palm of our hands.

Bad habits,
Hard to break,
Interactions,
Hard to maintain.

At the end of the day,
The stranger next door,
Will be your guardian.
A friend to your need.

Spend a little more time,
Extend a friendly hand.
Try to understand,
Your guardian angel.

Magical Time of the Year

Million thoughts,
A thousand dreams.
Wishes unheard.

Magical time of the year,
As they all say,
Wishes come true.

Her wishes,
Left unsaid,
And left unmade.

Happiness,
All but a myth.
Family: all but a treat.

They say,
Love life.
Smile more.

How can she?
All alone,
Supposedly magical.

Dark clouds of wishes,
Thunderous desires.

Her mind struggles to cope.

Screaming,
Sobbing,
Storming out.

High up,
Safe but unsafe
From her delirious mind.

Death loiters above and below;
She is in limbo.
Far away from lingering death.

Brave,
Yet weak.
That is true magic.

The Choice is Mine

I will never pick loneliness.
Say what you will;
The choice is mine.
It's a hard decision but,
I may need human company
To get me through the downs of life
Although it may burn me and tear me apart;
At least I won't be alone.
If I pick companionship, however toxic,
I might finally be happy
However, there are always two sides of the coin.
There won't be mums to nag and friends to judge
No gut-wrenching pain from the ones I love
My heart will finally get a fair chance to heal.
I urge myself to think:
Is solitude really loneliness?

Note: Now read bottom up

Happy Endings

Happy endings,
The ones where the princess wins,
The prince is the prize,
And evil is destroyed.

You believe in those;
Wholeheartedly.
Waiting impatiently,
For your very own.

He laughs,
At your naïve conviction.
He shakes his head,
Endings are not the best part.

He prefers the spice,
The taste of the journey.
The impact of the ending,
Will be stronger after the struggles.

You nod, thinking hard.
Dawning with understanding;
To light a candle,
You must cast a shadow.

A Little Reminder

Too harsh on yourself.
Give yourself a break, you're okay.
Winning if you're breathing.

Garba, an Emotion

Garba, an emotion.

The freshness of the night is intoxicating,
The colours, music, and beautiful twirling.

My breath hitches as my feet dance along,
Following their own tune, somehow;
Coming together in a captivating symphony.

My favourite time of the year,
A time when no caste, no religion matters.
We come together to pray, to dance,
To share sheer happiness.

The energetic beats of the music ignite us,
A different kind of passion,
The one where you can't stand still.

You have to join in, twirl in harmony,
With your friends, or complete strangers.

Garba, an emotion.

Glossary:

Garba: a traditional Indian dance form that
originates from the state of Gujarat.

Under 25

The night is young.
Shaking my hair free,
Soaking in the cool breeze;
Eyes sparkle hopefully.
Under twenty five,
More of life still to go.

Word count: 25

Dusty Memories

A distant memory,
Reaching desperately.
She's gone,
It feels unreal.

Like a dusty box,
Making its place.
The dust settles,
Until it's hard to clear.

Unclear pictures,
Her love trickling out.
Like an hourglass,
Slowly running out.

She's here,
In our hearts;
Despite the settled dust.
She'll always have a place.